Cheese Pirates
Humorous rhymes for adult children

Cheese Pirates
Humorous rhymes for adult children

Sabrina P. Ramet

 An imprint of New Academia Publishing
Washington, DC

Copyright © 2010 by Sabrina P. Ramet

New Academia Publishing, 2011

All rights reserved. No part of this book may be reproduced or transmitted in any form or by any means, electronic or mechanical, including photocopying, recording, or by any information storage and retrieval system.

Printed in the United States of America

Library of Congress Control Number: 2010937256
ISBN 978-0-9823867-8-1 paperback (alk. paper)

An imprint of new Academia Publishing
P.O. Box 27420, Washington, DC 20038-7420

info@newacademia.com
www.newacademia.com

For the Café Bombshell players:
Christine Hassenstab
Zachary T. Irwin,
Mills Kelly,
and Jerry Pankhurst,
whose acting abilities impressed us all…

Contents

Preface   xiii

Silly songs & political rhymes

Tick tack tock	3
Larry and Lucy	5
Lathe operator	7
Trofim Lysenko—anti-geneticist with a cause	8
Hero of Socialist Labor	10
Walpurgisnacht	11
Rat-ta-ta-tat	13
Surprise Witness	14
The moss inspectors come around	15
Cheese pirates	17
Putin on the moon	19
Down with tool revisionism	21
The Christmas fish	22
The Sheriff	24
Nun, but the lonely heart	27
A message from the Minnesota tourist bureau	29
Cast your vote for me	31
Seventeen cowboys	33

Bring back my Bonnie to me — zombie version	34
Monolithic theory of the state	35
Everybody must get stone	37
One-tonner meadow	38
Sponge salesman	39

American history in verse

A limerick history of the United States	43
Washington at Valley Forge	57
Carpet baggers	58
William Walker, King of Nicaragua	59
Jingle Ford	63
Fighting crime in Indiana, 1907	64
Warren G. Harding's teapot	66
Hero of Capitalist Labor	68
Fighting communism in the 1950s	69
J. Edgar Hoover's coming to town	70
Regime changer	72
Take me out to the war games	74

Bunnies, kitties, crocodiles

Rhyme of the Ancient Bunny	77
Sasha's song	79
Possible rabbits in this house	80
All aboard, kitties!	81
My cat's obsession	83
Do crocodiles have ghosts?	84
There's a rabbit in my brain	86

World history in rhyme

Gallia est omnis divisa	91
Hafizullah Amin's flies	93
Lukashenko's hippo	94
Cardinal Richelieu's cattery	95
Suleyman and his gazehounds go to Vienna for dinner	97
The falcons of Charles V	98
Twinkle, twinkle, Father Tsar	100
Enver, don't shoot	101
Honky-tonk Slobo	103
The red-capped cardinal and his pretty shark	105
Saparmurat Niazov Turkmenbashi's orchard of unicorns	106
Goebbels' Nazi turkey	108
Cleopatra's sweetie	109
The golden words of Mao Zedong	110
Die gute Zeiten rollen lassen	111
Bolsheviks vs. Mensheviks	113
Think of Stalin	115
Borut Pahor thanks Muammar al-Qaddafi for the gift of two camels	116
We all live on a great collective farm	117

Poems

War with the Tsar of Russia	121
Iskandar rise!	122
Justice	123
The extinction (2007)	124
Absolute Cheese	125
Real joy	126

Reggae

Ba-ba-daah	129
Reggae archaeologicae	130

Social commentary & ordinary life

The whole world's an ashtray	135
Forms	136
At the chemist's	137
Pleasantville, USA	138
Stopgap, Kansas	140
Building without mold	141
A sunset on velvet	143
Can a comrade be a gentleman?	144

The Shakespeare section

Who was it what wrote Shakespeare?	147
Breakfast with Shakespeare	148
Hamlet's soliloquy, revised & in rhyme	150
What if Shakespeare never was	151
Oh, Shakespeare was a poet	152

For the young at heart

Lions and tigers	157
Utensils	158
A lesson about life	159
Jacket and sweater	160
Recipe for Wiener Schnitzel	162

Something in my nose	163
A little story	164
Said the thrush to the shrew	166
Dandelions	167
Love birds	168
The expectorator	169
How absurd	170
The Washington D.C. metro system	171
Marches are what life's about	172

"Lathe operator" and "The whole world's an ashtray" are included in the author's novel, *Café Bombshell*, published by Scarith Books in 2008.

Illustrations

Trofim Lysenko	9
Walpurgisnacht	12
The Christmas fish	23
A message from the Minnesota tourist bureau	30
Captain Kangaroo	52
Nixon	53
Warren G. Harding's teapot	67
All aboard, kitties!	82
Do crocodiles have ghosts?	85
There's a rabbit in my brain	87
Lukashenka's hippo	94
Enver, don't shoot	102
Honky-tonk Slobo	104
Saparmurat Niazov Turkmenbashi's orchard of unicorns	107
Borut Pahor thanks Muammar al-Qaddafi for the gift of two camels	116
Forms	136
Something in my nose	163
Dandelions	167

All illustrations are courtesy of the artist, Christine M. Hassenstab.

Preface

I write rhymes and verse mainly to entertain myself and secondarily to entertain my friends and my classes. Almost all of the verse included in this collection was written between June 2007 and June 2010. The sole exception is "Rhyme of the Ancient Bunny" composed at least ten years earlier, although "The Extinction" and "How absurd" are reconstructions from memory of verse I had written as long as 40 years ago. Two of the rhymes included in this collection —"Lathe operator" and "The whole world's an ashtray"—were included in the author's novella, *Café Bombshell: The International Brain Surgery Conspiracy*, published by Scarith Books in 2008. I am grateful to Christine Hassenstab, Jennifer Bailey, Torbjørn Knutsen, Mikhail Gradovski, and Jason Hassenstab for feedback on the first drafts of some of the verse included herein, and to Jennifer Bailey, Sarah Correia, Christine Hassenstab, Torbjørn Knutsen, and Priscilla Ringrose for feedback on a later draft.

Sabrina P. Ramet
Trondheim, 13 June 2010

Silly songs & political rhymes

Tick tack tock

Tick tack tock
Traitors in the dock
Let release the guillotine
Tick tack tock.

Now Robespierre was fair,
But also doctrinaire:
He thought that revolution
Could not be laissez faire.

He thought that Danton's lot
Were mixed up in a plot,
He thought the nation's traitors
Earned the punishment they got.

Tick tack tock
Traitors in the dock
Let release the guillotine
Tick tack tock.

But Marat, he was Swiss
And had diathesis
It meant he had a skin disease
In every orifice.

And every day he read
Another order to behead,

'til he was stabbed while bathing
And was dead dead dead.

Tick tack tock
Traitors in the dock
Let release the guillotine
Tick tack tock.

It shows no disrespect
To do all to protect
The state and all its citizens
From the royal sect.

So sharpen up the blade
We have a renegade
Whose time is up, it's time to chop
So justice is repaid!

Tick tack tock
Traitors in the dock
Let release the guillotine
Tick tack tock.

Larry and Lucy

Larry and Lucy were lovers
They liked to lie in the lounge
They licked their licorice loudly
And looked at lingerie
Leather is love
You learn to fly high above.

Orville and Ornice liked orgies
They ordered orchids or else
They sat around in the orchard
And discussed their past ordeals.
Original orbs
Are much rounder than chords.

Rory and Rosie were racers
They revved their Rolls to a roar
They really relished the rivalry
And rarely showed remorse.
Racing is right
You've got to stay with the fight.

Clara and Clarence were clever
They cloned a chick with a click
They reached a classical climax
But they clubbed the climate down
Temperatures climb
Will we run out of time?

Peggy and Perry liked petting
They put the pastries aside
They spent a week on the pillow
Just petting 'round the clock
This news just filed:
They say that petting is wild.

Fergie and Filbert felt funny
They found a file full of fibs
Off in the other dimension
They frolicked with the folks.
Folly is false,
You can dance to a waltz.

Lathe operator

I wake up in the mornin' an' get out of bed
I feel so sleepy that I feel half dead
I brush ma teeth an' I scrub ma head
Gotta get ma coffee an' a piece of bread.
I jump in the tub an' start my bathin'
But I can't wait to do some lathin'.
Cause I'm a lathe operator
A lathe operator
When I turn on my lathe, I'm on top of the world
Cause I'm a lathe operator,
I'm a lathe operator an' I just can't get enough.

I work ma shift an' I'm done at five
Then I get in ma car an' I start to drive
Tomorrow I'll be back for another eight,
I wanna get up early so I won't be late.
Cause whatever I do I'm always cravin'
To get back to work and do some lathin'
Cause I'm a lathe operator
A lathe operator
When I turn on my lathe, I'm on top of the world
Cause I'm a lathe operator,
I'm a lathe operator an' I just can't get enough.

Trofim Lysenko – anti-geneticist with a cause

Everybody knows that I am what you see
I can make a carrot grow as big as a tree
I can make a cantaloupe that fills up the sea
It's time that you admit that you're indebted to me.

Give me a prize
for vegetable size
Give me a toot
for the size of your fruit.

Trofim Lysenko – that is my name
Making crops grow bigger is the name of the game
Genetics is a lie, you can be what you will
Down with Charlie Darwin 'cause he's over the hill.

Give me a toast
just let me boast
Of all of my deeds
and for meeting your needs.

Everybody knows .... La – la – la
Trofim Lysenko .... La – la – la
Down with genetics .... La – la – la
Crops growing bigger .... La – la – la
La – la – la, la – la – la.
Trofim Lysenko – that is my name!

Hero of Socialist Labor

I can mine a hundred tons of coal per shift
I've got muscle and there's tons that I can lift
My hero is Stakhanov
He's obviously a one-off
I can mine a hundred tons of coal per shift.

Aleksei Stakhanov mined a hundred eight
Back in 1935 he pulled his weight
My hero is Stakhanov
He's obviously a one-off
Aleksei Stakhanov mined a hundred eight.

He set records that will stand the test of time
And he did it when no longer in his prime
Hey, my hero is Stakhanov
He's obviously a one-off
He set records that will stand the test of time.

Walpurgisnacht

Every year on the eve of May
Witches dance and salute the day
They make magic, they cast spells
Just don't ring those steeple bells!
It's the Witches' Sabbath,
Better celebrate!

Demonic possession – just say no!
Tell the devil he should go
Back to his home in the depths of hell
And tell him to take his awful smell.
It's the Witches' Sabbath,
Better celebrate!

If you go inside the sphinx
You will find that the whole place stinks,
That's because of the mummy's curse –
It just makes everything smell much worse.
It's the Witches' Sabbath,
Better celebrate!

If the devil's in your head,
And you see the walking dead,
You might think that you're insane –
Time to purify your brain!
It's the Witches' Sabbath,
Better celebrate!

When the clock tolls twelve the witches count
How many come to Brocken Mount,
How many spirits stay behind,
How much evil invades the mind.
It's the Witches' Sabbath,
Better celebrate!

Rat-ta-ta-tat

Rat-ta-ta-tat tat
Rat-ta-ta-tat tat
The drummers are coming
The bugles are coming
The muskets are coming
The colonels are coming
Rat-ta-ta-tat tat.

Rat-ta-ta-tat tat
Rat-ta-ta-tat tat
The fight will be gory
They're fighting for glory
Each man has his story
The enemy's hoary
Rat-ta-ta-tat tat.

Rat-ta-ta-tat tat
Rat-ta-ta-tat tat
There's no need to worry
We'll make our foe sorry
The rifles are coming
The cannon are coming
Rat-ta-ta-tat tat.

Surprise Witness

Have you ever seen
Such a huge squeezed lime?
Must have been around
And have witnessed the crime.
Get its testimony
Gotta write it down.
Don't allow the citrus
To go out of town.
When we go to trial
We'll plan to utilize
Our eye-witness lime:
The defense will be surprised!

The moss inspectors come around

(May be sung to the tune of "When Johnny Comes Marching Home Again")

The moss inspectors come around
Hurrah! Hurrah!
They measure the moss that's on the ground
Hurrah! Hurrah!
And if they find it weighs more than a pound
Then you'll find that you're legally bound
To pay fees and fines on all of the moss you got.

The mold inspectors check for mold
Hurrah! Hurrah!
All of them, why they've been told
Hurrah! Hurrah!
To check all the ketchup for signs of mold
And scoop out the bad parts before it is sold
So we all get mold-free ketchup with what we got.

The tax collectors make mistakes
Hurrah! Hurrah!
Don't be expecting any breaks!
Hurrah! Hurrah!
And when you see what the tax man makes
You'll be pleased with whatever he takes,
So be glad, not mad, when taxes go up – or down.

The book reviewers don't read books
Hurrah! Hurrah!
They judge your book by how it looks
Hurrah! Hurrah!
And if it is thin and not too thick
And if they are healthy and not too sick,
Then they'll just complain 'bout what's not in your book.

Cheese pirates

They sail across the oceans, merry men,
Pirates, if you please,
Who do not crave riches or power,
But wish only for cheese.
When they board ocean liners,
And from their scabbards pull their blades,
They only seek the stocks of cheese.
So there's no need to feel afraid.
They like to talk about "land lubbers",
"Ahoy, m'hearties" they like to cry.
But when they ask to see your cheese,
You'd be well advised to comply.
"There'll be no killin' 'til I give the word,"
Their captain mumbles in an alcoholic daze,
But he is only reading from a script:
His words date from his cinematic phase.
No one has ever felt their blade
Or been shot by any of their crew,
They are a harmless lot, I tell you,
And everything I tell of them is true.
And as their ship disappears into the horizon,
And as the day grows long,
If you cup your ears and listen hard,
You may hear the cheese pirates sing their song:
"Yo-ho, yo-ho, a block of cheese for me,
I'll settle for some Roquefort, a cheddar or a brie.

I always bring some bread along
Because I have a hunch,
That there'll be cheese for taking –
And that means time for lunch."

Putin on the moon

The US thinks they've won the race –
the first man on the moon –
but Putin knows that outer space
can play to Moscow's tune.

No head of state has gone to Mars
or through the Milky Way
but Putin plans to see the stars
and put on a display.

The public has a gnawing thirst
for something new and more;
so Putin plans to be the first
as head of state to soar

To distant stars and planets
and circle 'round the sun,
intent to show the world below
that Russia's number one.

But Putin's ship is thrown off course
because it launched too soon,
and Russia's leader finds he's forced
to settle for the moon.

He finds the stars and stripes are there
and hurls it to the ground,
and plants a Russian flag instead,
then starts to look around.

Putin now comes on the air,
the Russians ought to know:
Aside from him the moon is bare,
there's no place here to go.

"So if you want a party,
you're better off at home,"
he tells his people honestly,
"'cause here you're all alone."

But weightlessness is kinda cool,
so Putin leaps and skips,
before he packs his bag and leaves
to fly back on his ship.

Down with tool revisionism!

The pen is mightier than the tractor
   when you want to write a letter
The tractor is mightier than the pen
   when you want to plow a field
Don't use a tractor as a writing implement
Don't use a pen to plow a field
Use every tool for its assigned purpose
Down with tool revisionism!

The Christmas fish

Bring out the dish
with the Yuletide fish
It's Christmas time again!
Fill up my glass
with a slug of kvas
It's Christmas time again!

He's looking at me, the Christmas fish
What could he be thinking?
You say he's dead –well, are you sure?
Hey look, I think he's winking!

We've worked all year in the lumber yards
Doin' lots of labor
And what we want to do is eat
And sing some songs with neighbors.

Bring out the dish
with the Yuletide fish
It's Christmas time again!
Fill up my glass
with a slug of kvas
It's Christmas time again!

Choppin' down trees is lots of work
But it's a worthwhile action,
'cause when you're done you see results
And that brings satisfaction.

You work real hard and sweat real hard,
And that means perspiration,
But choppin' trees is heaven's work
It'll save you from damnation!

*Bring out the dish
with the Yuletide fish
It's Christmas time again!
Fill up my glass
with a slug of kvas
It's Christmas time again!*

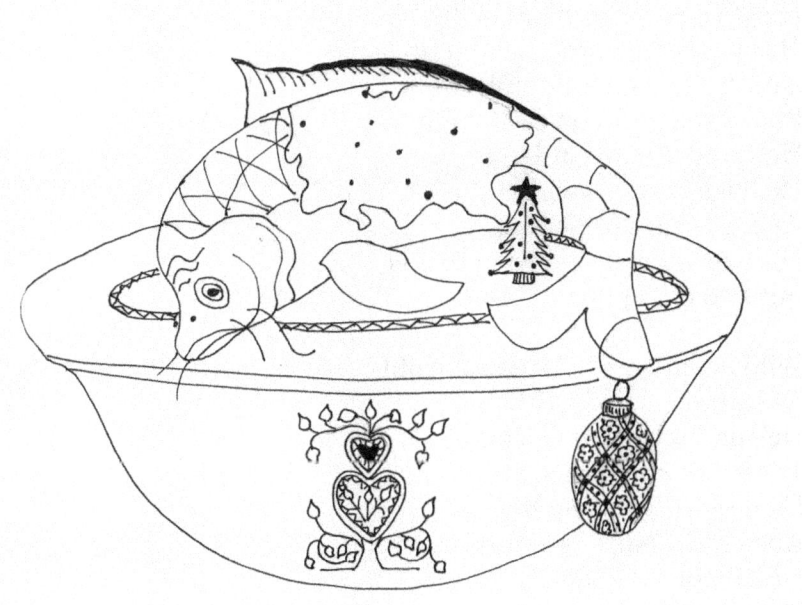

The Sheriff

The Sheriff polishes his cattlehide boots
And buttons up his shirt and vest,
He puts his pants on by himself.
He's the fastest gun out in the West.
He knows that outlaws hold up banks
And rustlers go for cattle,
But with a pistol on each thigh,
He's ready to do battle.
He dons his fancy Gucci shades,
And grabs his Miller hat,
His hair is neatly coiled in braids
But also full of gnats.

With nostrils wide he gets a whiff
Of scandal in the court
He's on his bronco in a jiff,
There's trouble to abort.
He ties his bronco to the rail
And crashes through the door,
He cannot show that he is frail,
He cannot be a bore.
He passes through the foyers,
This must be a surprise!
He must restrain the lawyers
Who are telling endless lies.

And now he's in the courtroom,
His water pistols blazing,
The full effect that he achieves
Is really quite amazing.
The lawyers very soon are soaked
The judge has gone to sleep,
The jury may as well have croaked –
They sit like bleatless sheep.
"I do declare a mistrial,"
He shouts in perfect Greek,
"The evidence is false and vile."
The judge shows off his great physique.

The jurors file in silence
And leave the court behind,
They've heard about some violence,
And now need to unwind
They wander to the city bar,
And order rounds of beer,
They figure if they drink enough
It all will seem quite clear.
The sheriff is so proud and pleased
With what he's done this day,
He gives himself a medal,
And buys himself a holiday.

He's the fastest gun out in the West
He closes all his cases,
He's smart, he's strong, he is the best,
He always wins his chases.
There should be films about him –
Of that he is quite sure.
He's ready to go to Hollywood
And then to go on tour.
"Oh make a film about me,
I'm fabulous and great,
You can't do without me,"
He does most clearly state.

And so he waits for destiny,
For fame must surely come,
He bites his nails, fate will prevail,
His mind is going numb.

Nun, but the lonely heart

There was a nun called Bernadette
her friends all called her Bern,
She hoped to be the new popette
since it was women's turn.
For now she was superior,
the nuns all called her Mother,
But passion burned inside her heart
her dreams were of another.
Bern baby Bern
no point in being lonely,
Bern baby Bern
the heart is feeling moanly.

In Sea Forth – that's a nearby town –
there were two friendly priests
who liked to have her over
for Friday evening feasts.
They went across the border
to Canada and danced,
and then she left the order
and continued the romance.
Bern baby Bern
Two priests are better than one
Bern baby Bern
Not lonely now ex-nun.

They settled down in River Falls
they didn't want to tarry,
but which of these two priestly folk
should she choose to marry?
She finally decided that
it was too hard to choose,
So better to stay celibate
and all sex refuse.
Bern baby Bern
Abstinence is best,
Bern baby Bern,
Nun – you've passed the test.

A message from the Minnesota tourist bureau

In almost every place we've been,
that we recall, at least,
the sunset's always in the west
and sunrise in the east.
But it's the other way around
on Minnesota's farms,
where crimson sunsets in the west
can stir some real alarm.

In other states, we've heard it told,
it is the dogs that bark,
while cats will purr and sometimes meow
and cling onto the bark.
But here in Minneapolis
it is the dogs that meow
and cats that chase the postman
and bark and say bow-wow.

In other lands and cities,
you sit down on your chair,
but here in Minnesota
you're floating in the air.
At breakfast, lunch and dinner
the food is floating by,
it's lighter than the air you breathe
and you are flying high.

So visit Minnesota
enjoy our special shade.
You won't be disappointed,
no need to be afraid.
So just come on 'round and visit us!

Cast your vote for me

(may be sung to the tune of "By a waterfall" by Busby Berkeley for the film "Footlight Parade" (1933) and first sung by Dick Powell)

Cast your vote for me
I'll work for you-hoo-hoo-hoo
If you vote for me,
that's best for you-hoo-hoo-hoo
It'll be a heavenly day
I promise I'll double your pay.

Problems can be solved,
Your dreams come true-hoo-hoo-hoo
If you will elect
me and my crew.
It's a happy honeymoon,
it's very catchy tune,
if you sing along with me.

Cast your vote for me
I'll work for you-hoo-hoo-hoo
If you vote for me
that's best for you-hoo-hoo-hoo.
We'll keep the prices so low
You'll see your wages will really grow.

Problems can be solved,
Your dreams come true-hoo-hoo-hoo
If you will elect
me and my crew.
It's election time again,

let me try to make this plain:
I can make your dreams
come true…

Seventeen cowboys

(Inspired by the melody of Stephen Collins Foster's "Beautiful Dreamer", and with not-so-subtle allusions to Karl Marx's "German Ideology")

Seventeen cowboys up on a hill,
packin' some whiskey, takin' a swill,
brandin' some cattle, yodeling too,
if you could join them, now wouldn't you?

Finding a clearing, soon they will stop,
build a few cabins, settin' up shop,
fetchin' a guí-tar, strummin' some chords,
livin' like this and no one gets bored.

Hunt in the mornin', then you go fish,
rear cattle near evenin', food on the dish,
then you can criticize, after your meal,
say what you're thinkin', whatever you feel.

The problem is money – there just ain't enough,
them folks that got it, treatin' us rough.
Time is a-comin' when cowboys will ride,
and lasso the bossman, tannin' his hide.

Bring back my Bonnie to me – zombie version

(to be sung to the tune of "My Bonnie lies over the ocean", a traditional Scottish folk song)

My Bonnie was buried last Tuesday
her coffin lies under a mound
but some folks can dig up your loved ones
and bring them back out of the ground.

Bring back, bring back, oh bring back my Bonnie to me, to me,
Bring back, bring back, oh bring back my Bonnie to me.

I know that she might be a zombie
her brain will no longer be right,
she's scratchin' away at the coffin,
once out she will look quite a fright.

Bring back, bring back, oh bring back my Bonnie to me, to me,
Bring back, bring back, oh bring back my Bonnie to me.

Oh come on guys, help with the shovel,
please dig away some of the dirt,
my zombie-girl may still be breathing,
I'm sure that she's not yet inert.

Bring back, bring back, oh bring back my Bonnie to me, to me,
Bring back, bring back, oh bring back my Bonnie to me.

Monolithic theory of the state

(to be sung to the tune of "Polly Wolly Doodle", a nineteenth-century American song written by Daniel Emmett)

Oh, I flew out east to old Pyongyang
sing monolithic theory of the state,
'cause I think I'm likin' Kim Jong-il
sing monolithic theory of the state.

Fare thee well, fare thee well,
'cause I want to dee-fect now,
'cause the DMZ looks wider when you're already inside 'er
sing monolithic theory of the state.

Now chuch'e is a good idea
sing monolithic theory of the state,
it brings new wisdom, makes life clear,
sing monolithic theory of the state.

Fare thee well, fare thee well,
'cause I want to dee-fect now,
'cause the DMZ looks wider when you're already inside 'er
sing monolithic theory of the state.

Oh the leader-dear has banished fear
sing monolithic theory of the state,
and I must obey what he will say,
sing monolithic theory of the state.

Fare thee well, fare thee well,
'cause I want to dee-fect now,
'cause the DMZ looks wider when you're already inside 'er
sing monolithic theory of the state.

Everybody must get stone

If you want a pizza of your very own
you gotta put the pizza on a pizza stone.
This is something you can buy in any pizza shop,
just tell them that you want a stone to lay your dough on top.
Everybody must, everybody must, everybody must get stone.

Don't believe it if you're told that you can make it work
without a stone 'cause if you try, your pizza'll go beserk.
No, listen what I tell you in a very solemn tone:
If you wanna make a pizza, then you gotta get a stone.
Everybody must, everybody must, everybody must get stone.

If you like a pizza, then you gotta like a cheese,
garlic and tomatoes and a pepper if you please,
just put 'em on a pizza dough that's lying on the stone,
you make delicious pizza and you never eat alone.
Everybody must, everybody must, everybody must get stone.

One-tonner meadow

One-tonner meadow, why here's a one-tonner meadow,
One-tonner meadow, why here's a one-tonner meadow.

So you got a one-ton truck,
see you find you are in luck,
on the meadow you can drive
and you see you will survive,
but bring a two-ton truck around,
and you'll sink right down down down.
'cause it's a one-tonner meadow,
why it's a one-tonner meadow,
one-tonner meadow,
why here's a one-tonner meadow.

Bring a three-ton truck on ground –
man, you crazy: you go down!
Your thinking must be sickly,
an' you sinking oh so quickly,
but a one-ton truck's OK,
you can drive on the field all day,
'cause it's a one-tonner meadow,
why it's a one-tonner meadow,
one-tonner meadow,
why here's a one-tonner meadow.
One-tonner meadow,
why here's a one-tonner meadow…

Sponge salesman

He walks the streets with his head held high,
proud of his calling, my oh my,
He sells sponges – that's his job –
and he's got a great supply.
Sponge salesman, sponge salesman!
That's the job for him!

When he was just a little boy,
of all his playthings his best toy
was a little squishy sponge –
that was something to enjoy!
Sponge salesman, sponge salesman!
That's the job for him!

When he was only six years old,
he went to his mamma whom he told,
"Mamma, sponges – they are great,
soft and squishy and they clean up mold!"
Sponge salesman, sponge salesman!
That's the job for him!

So he went on to sponging school,
studied sponge science and the laws and rules,
graduated at the top of his class,
when it comes to sponges, he's no fool!
Sponge salesman, sponge salesman!
That's the job for him!

He landed a job at the edge of town,
selling sponges up and down,
selling sponges right and left,
soon acquired some great renown.
Sponge salesman, sponge salesman!
That's the job for him!

It's the safest job on the planet – yes!
In that I trust you'll acquiesce,
you can bang your head on any sponge –
it will cause you no distress.
Sponge salesman, sponge salesman!
That's the job for him!

In his work he feels fulfilled,
knowing that his sponges have thrilled
many a mademoiselle and gent
and helped to clean up liquids spilled.
Sponge salesman, sponge salesman!
That's the job for him!
Oh, sponge salesman, sponge salesman!
That's the job for him!

American history in verse

A limerick history of the United States

"We've told you again and again,"
Said the wise men of England and Spain,
"that the planet is flat,
It's as simple as that.
So desist from your round-earth refrain."

But Columbus thought he knew the best
And he promised that if he sailed west,
He would land in the east,
And what mattered the least
Was what all the wise men had guessed.

So the king and the queen said "Okay,
We'll give you three ships and we'll pay
For supplies and a crew
So that you all can do
All the things that we've both heard you say."

But Columbus found to his dismay
There were lands that had got in his way,
So he claimed them for Spain
And he sailed home again
To be feted by shouts of "Hurray!"

The New World was soon in the news
And people were lining in queues
They wanted to be

Where the sun meets the sea,
And they felt they had nothing to lose.

There were pilgrims in bonnets and hats,
Who arrived and constructed some flats.
It wasn't too long
'til they burst out in song,
To rejoice in their new habitats.

They invited the Indians to dine,
Eating turkey with carrots and wine,
And they all gave a cheer
'cause Thanksgiving was here,
And agreed that the dinner was fine.

But the English imposed lots of tax
That was straining and breaking the backs
Of the patriots who
Thought the tax was a clue
That the time had arrived for an ax.

They felt it was time to resist
And they sent out a call to enlist
In the Army of George
In the cold Valley Forge.
But to win they would have to persist.

They selected the Fourth of July
To announce that they would now rely
On the musket and sword –
Throw the tea overboard! –
Now was the time to defy!

George Washington felt somewhat skittish
He knew that his foe was the British
But through battle and din
He knew he would win,
'cause his soldiers were well trained and fittish.

The colonists rose to the test
With an eagle affixed to their crest,
All they wanted to be
Was courageous and free,
And to blaze a trail out to the West.

While Napoleon's brigadiers fought,
From the French Thomas Jefferson bought,
A slice of terrain –
Now that was a gain!
And the price was not much above naught.

James Polk is remembered as strong
'cause he didn't pay heed to the throng
He annexed more land,
To the great Rio Grand,
To the "Manifest Destiny" song.

But some differences started dividing
The South from the North that was chiding
The holders of slaves
While they fought with the braves,
And the quarreling wasn't subsiding.

A Civil War started and flared,
And the pain and the violence were shared,
It lasted four years,
Bringing sadness and tears,
And the soul of the nation was bared.

Abe Lincoln won much adulation,
He knew how to give an oration,
But once he was dead –
He'd been shot in the head –
There was sadness throughout the nation.

But the Yankees invented the thresher
And how to make popcorn taste fresher,

The paint tube and phone,
The spray gun and clone,
Were results of American pressure.

The cotton gin combed up the cotton,
And the fridge keeps food not going rotten,
But the greatest of all,
In the USA's haul,
Is what some folks have nearly forgotten.

I'm thinking of bright roller skates,
The inventor himself demonstrates:
Jim Plimpton would say,
For a fast get-away,
Eight wheels on your feet defy fate.

But the treatment of Indians was brutal,
And their weapons proved rather inutile,
They were crushed and were killed,
Their life's blood was spilled,
Their every resistance was futile.

Then gold was discovered –hurray!
On John Sutter's farm– lackaday!
But that didn't stop those
Who presumed to suppose
That they might haul John's gold away.

The railroads were built – it was thought –
So that people could go where they ought,
And not feel distraught
Or the least overwrought
That they'd fail in what they had been taught.

Ulysses S. Grant knew that schools
were good educational tools,
He put state schools in place
and the US kept pace,
Yes President Grant was no fool.

The next twenty years were quite boring,
politicians were sleeping and snoring.
It was left to the banks
and their lick-spittle cranks
to assure that their riches were soaring.

Eventually old Bill McKinley
ran for office and then he did winley,
"My boots I must shine,
'cause the White House is mine,"
he said while he was moving in-ly.

McKinley found life was a bore,
For excitement he wanted a war.
So he blew up the Maine
and blamed it on Spain,
and with that his spirits did soar.

The Spanish said "Take what you want.
We are feeble and tired and gaunt.
Just don't start a war
Please take Cuba and more,
We won't even protest or taunt."

But McKinley was praying to God
Who told him that something was odd
if the Spanish seemed filled
with a dread they'd be killed,
And with that he proceeded to nod.

American forces broke through,
Taking Cuba and Philippines too,
The Spanish lost ships,
While pursing their lips.
Hurrah for the red, white, and blue!

But later McKinley was shot
And instantly died on the spot

Teddy Roosevelt now
Took the oath and a vow
That as president he'd do a lot.

He opened the national parks
On history he left his mark.
He busted some trusts,
He knew that he must,
And led the land out of the dark.

To sail from New York to LA
was taking a week and a day,
So they built a canal
-- though it sounds so banal –
right where Panama stood in the way.

But Americans soon were aghast,
As Europe was sliding quite fast
Into quarrels and fights
Over dynastic rights
And who should be second from last.

Sarajevo was where it all started,
When the Archduke of Habsburg was martyred.
He was taking a ride
With his wife at his side,
When he came to be called "the departed".

The war which ensued was quite vicious,
With submarines quite surreptious
Whether English or Russians
Or Frenchmen or Prussians,
All parties were very ambitious.

But America stood proud and tall,
Woodrow Wilson spoke out with this call,
"I've done what I can
With a 14-point plan,
To bring justice and fairness to all."

War ended and then came the days
Of a most isolationist phase
There were songs in the air
People had not a care,
And indulged in the Charleston dance craze.

But congressmen were in a funk,
Knowing some people liked to get drunk.
They thought this would end,
If they just could amend
The law of the land – it was bunk.

Prohibition could never succeed,
Alcohol filled a deep human need
Or so it was thought
By all those who bought
Moonshine or bottles of mead.

Black Friday changed all this obsession,
America faced a recession
People lined up for soup
While the young Betty Boop
Tried to relieve their depression.

On Wall Street there was such a panic
when banks and investors went manic,
the economy crashed
and job slots were slashed –
it was just like another Titanic.

Herb Hoover was blamed for the flop
And lost his job up at the top,
And FDR came
And established his fame
As the man who made misery stop.

In Congress there was much dissension
'bout whether to give people pensions,

But F. Roosevelt signed
Just a bill of this kind --
That tranquilized many a tension.

Then Hitler arrived on the scene
And transformed the German routine,
He targeted Jews
Under some sort of ruse,
Nazi thinking was really obscene.

The Nazis decided on war,
Carved up Poland and still wanted more,
They occupied France
And then took a chance,
Russia was what they craved for.

On 7 December, ill day,
The Japanese struck U. S. A.
At Pearl Harbor the ships
Were attacked and did flips,
And the harbor was in disarray.

So America knew it must act
To conquer the New Order pact,
'twas a battle of wills,
The good against ill,
So let patriots rise and react.

The cause of the just then prevailed,
And the Nazis and Fascists – they failed.
They were taken to court,
Where most came up short,
And were taken to prison and jailed.

America proved to be swift
with the great Marshall Plan as a gift,
The money would aid
to reverse Europe's fade
and to give all its people a lift.

But the communists were on the take,
in East Europe and China to make
people go back to school
for one-party rule.
It was a political quake.

Joe McCarthy knew this could be bad,
The whole world was acting so mad
He thought communists were
like a wolf in cat's fur,
and that made McCarthy feel sad.

So he set up committees to seek
to distinguish the reds from the meek,
Un-American acts
were important as facts
as the campaign was pushed week to week.

But the Sputnik was first into space,
with the Russians ahead in the race
to get to the moon
so that they could then croon
and use this to buttress their case.

The TV soon offered much more,
and the children would lie on the floor,
their eyes glued to the screen,
they enjoyed what they'd seen,
and wondered what still lay in store.

Dobie Gillis and all of his ilk
and Engineer Bill with his milk,
Larry, Moe, Curly Joe,
Perry Como and show,
Ann Southern all dressed up in silk.

"I love Lucy" was one of the first
and "I married Joan" quenched the thirst

for a comedy thrill
and you'll scarcely get ill
from watching "Three Sons" do their worst.

"The Phil Silvers show" was a hoot
Gomez Adams and Munsters to boot,
Captain Kangaroo's back
"Our Miss Brooks" is on track,
and Twilight Zone's ready to shoot.

Old President Ike was quite bald,
did not know that his country was stalled,
On the question of rights.
For blacks and for whites,
equality should be installed.

Then Ike's office term came to an end,
JFK came and promised to mend
all the problems he found,
Had his feet on the ground,
and his jogging would set a new trend

Jack Kennedy thought it was grand,
If a US-made spacecraft could land
On top of the moon,
Plant a flag in a dune,
And an astronaut walk in the sand.

Camelot – that was his palace,
But he died after visiting Dallas,
LBJ took the reins,
And he went to great pains,
To expunge all resentment and malice.

To do this he pushed civil rights,
And tried to end poverty's plight,
He earned people's cheers,
But after six years,
He retired and ended the fight.

After Johnson came Nixon and crew,
Who promised that they would undo
Some of LBJ's laws,
where they thought there were flaws,
What was best for the country they knew.

After four years in office the boss
was ahead in the polls by a toss,
but he worried too much
and needed a crutch
to be sure to avert a big loss.

So he hired some plumbers who went
down to Watergate where it was meant
they should bug the man's phone
so that it could be known
what went on in the Democrats' tent.

But the Washington Post blew the whistle,
The scandal blew up like a missile.
Nixon quickly denied
that his agents had spied,
they were just going 'round picking thistle.

Eventually Nixon resigned
but the incoming leader was kind:

Gerald Ford soon decided,
since Nixon'd been chided,
that an amnesty grant should be signed.

Jimmy Carter, a native of Plains,
felt that he had the talent and brains
to make the world just,
shouting "Freedom or bust!"
and proceeded to reach for the reins.

But Carter was out after four,
with a low popularity score,
an actor had won
and with Carter gone,
the Republicans minded the store.

Ronald Reagan – a cowboy and actor –
soon proved that he could be a factor –
the economy boomed
as he ended the gloom,
and came to be called "benefactor".

George Bush, as his veep, was robust
and was someone that Reagan could trust.
They made deals with Iran
'cause they figured Islam
would help Sandinistas go bust.

Ron Reagan was aging so fast
and his memory gradually passed,
so he got off his horse
and told Bush "Of course,
take over and fight to the last!"

George Bush's attention was turned
to the issue of flags being burned.
He showed his resolve
as he set out to solve
this problem which made him concerned.

The Soviets were in a pickle –
how to save the old hammer and sickle?
Their economy crashed
and the ruble was smashed,
and soon was worth less than a nickel.

But Yeltsin took over and danced,
And with that was his image enhanced.
He privatized fast,
Til he sold off the last
Of the properties Russia had chanced.

Bill Clinton made friends with Lewinsky
with whom he committed a sinsky,
The Republicans raged
while the president aged,
as he took all their blows on his chinsky.

Fidelity – that was the key
If you thought that you wanted to be
The commander-in-chief,
'cause the president's brief
Is to let all Americans see –

What a husband can be to his spouse,
When he's sitting at home in the house.
He should stay in his bed,
The Republicans said,
Or abandon the president's house.

A congressman named Henry Hyde
Thought that he was Republicans' pride,
So he sought to expose
Clinton's follies, and pose
As America's virtuous guide.

When terrorists struck the Twin Towers,
George W. Bush had the powers

to take things in hand
to protect the whole land,
from people to rabbits to flowers.

"I didn't grow up in the ocean,"
Said President Bush with emotion,
But "Wall Street got drunk,"
And slipped into a funk.
But Bush couldn't come up with a notion.

Some wanted their Bush to remain
as their boss 'cause they cherished his brain,
But the Texan went home
and Dick Cheney – the gnome –
retired feeling happy and sane.

Then Obama soared high in the hopes
of the people who gave him their votes.
Yes, we can – he would say,
and with that won the day:
in the USA "yeses", not "nopes".

You have now heard the USA story,
which is mostly not nasty or gory,
but a story of dreams
of what is what it seems,
of a nation that's striving for glory.

Washington at Valley Forge

Washington – now he was George,
Spent some time at Valley Forge
He was cold, he blew his nose,
Glad to have some winter clothes.

Five foot eight was how he stood
All his molars, made of wood
Father of his country and
Liked to hear a marching band.

Carpet baggers

Carpet baggers – that is us,
there's no need to make a fuss
We're just pleased to take control
and if you've got one, buy your soul.
Now it's time for Reconstruction:
that should serve for (an) introduction.
We've got carpets you can buy
don't tell us the price is high.

Up in Jersey, life is great
but we think it's not too late
for you rebels to be taught
respect for us and what we've brought.
We've brought carpets just for you,
bring your cash, get in the queue,
Carpet baggers – that is us,
there's no need to make a fuss.

William Walker, King of Nicaragua

A lad was born on the 8th of May
In eighteen hundred twenty four
His parents shouted "hip hooray!"
And tap-danced on the timber floor.
Young William Walker had some brains
And finished college at fourteen,
He went 'round Europe, riding trains,
All the while he was assorting
Ideas that he'd put to use
In the conquests that he planned
To see English more diffuse
-- it was the tongue at his command.

Refrain:

> *English should be the language of choice*
> *When Nicaraguans want to give voice*
> *To their opinions and to their conceptions.*
> *English should be the language of choice.*

He started with medicine, then he thought
he'd hang out his shingle as a fresh MD,
Then he changed his mind and took up law,
But soon came down with some bad ennui.
So he gathered rangers who swore they would
Practice conquests where they could.
In Mexico they began their trade,
Declared a republic and built a stockade.

Expanded refrain:

English should be the language of choice
When Nicaraguans want to give voice
To their opinions and to their conceptions.
English should be the language of choice.

Why speak in Spanish when you can choose
American English, which you can use
When you're in Boston or out in India?
English should be the language you use.

He talked with his men and they were sure
that Nicaraguans would be glad
to see them coming so demure;
they would know that Walker had
the means to end their slavery
and praise his virile bravery.

Re-expanded refrain:

English should be the language of choice
When Nicaraguans want to give voice
To their opinions and to their conceptions.
English should be the language of choice.

Why speak in Spanish when you can choose
American English, which you can use
When you're in Boston or out in India?
English should be the language you use.

If you speak English, everyone knows
The point of the sentences that you compose.
Why be content to be not understood,
When you have English, which everyone knows?

Walker and company marched and marched,
Their stomachs ached, their mouths were parched.
But they beat the army, won their goal,
And in the country took control.

Further expanded refrain:

> *English should be the language of choice*
> *When Nicaraguans want to give voice*
> *To their opinions and to their conceptions.*
> *English should be the language of choice.*
>
> *Why speak in Spanish when you can choose*
> *American English, which you can use*
> *When you're in Boston or out in India?*
> *English should be the language you use.*
>
> *If you speak English, everyone knows*
> *The point of the sentences that you compose.*
> *Why be content to be not understood,*
> *When you have English, which everyone knows?*
>
> *Time to be strong, not to be weak,*
> *So pass a law to make everyone speak*
> *The language you like 'cause you know that it is,*
> *Time to be strong, not to be weak.*

Walker established himself as a king
Of fair Nicaragua – that was the thing.
For three years he reigned and everyone cheered
For this clean-shaven man with no moustache or beard!
But then the Hondurans captured this guy,
They pummeled his bottom and they made him cry,
They brought out the rifles while he held his breath,
That was the day that he met his death.

Final refrain:

*English should be the language of choice
When Nicaraguans want to give voice
To their opinions and to their conceptions.
English should be the language of choice.*

*Why speak in Spanish when you can choose
American English, which you can use
When you're in Boston or out in India?
English should be the language you use.*

Jingle Ford

Henry Ford, Henry Ford
in his motorcar
He's packed a lunch with sandwiches
and some caviar.

Hey, watch him drive, watch him drive,
while he's shifting gears:
You can see he feels alive
in spite of all his years.

Honking on his horn,
never weatherworn,
Steers the steering wheel
keeps the car on keel.
With this new device,
he's risen to the top.
Since there are no traffic lights
he'll never have to stop.

Oh,
Henry Ford, Henry Ford
in his motorcar
He's packed a lunch with sandwiches
and some caviar.

Hey, watch him drive, watch him drive,
while he's shifting gears:
You can see he feels alive
in spite of all his years.

Fighting crime in Indiana, 1907

Indiana was a happy state
Except for all the lawyers
Who badgered each other daily
While standing in the foyers.
They thought that there was too much crime
And blamed it on "defectives"
And then they cursed and grumbled
And shouted out invectives.

Refrain:
"Three generations of idiots
Is nearly and really enough,
It's time to get serious and fix it,
It's time that we start to get tough."

The lawyers met and all agreed
To contact Dr. Sharp,
A medical man of pedigree
To whom they liked to carp.
Inventor of vasectomy,
The cutting edge of science,
Old Dr. Sharp was highly trained
And had a surgeon's license.

Refrain:
"Three generations of idiots
Is nearly and really enough,

It's time to get serious and fix it,
It's time that we start to get tough."

The doctor knew crime could be beaten
By cutting away certain parts,
His energy seemed almost boundless
He was easily ready to start.
Judge Law thought that Sharp was on target
And said, "Let the cutting begin,"
And as he began the procedures,
The medical doctor would sing:

Refrain:
"Three generations of idiots
Is nearly and really enough,
It's time to get serious and fix it,
It's time that we start to get tough."

Warren G. Harding's teapot

Warren G. Harding liked to drink tea
Teapot and biscuits by the sea
But he didn't like to drink alone
So he built himself a Teapot Dome.
Warren – you please me so,
And you let the good times flow.

One lump or two lumps, as you please,
Add a little scandal and a lot of sleaze,
If you've got a government
Corruption is its fundament.
Warren – I like your hair,
And you look so debonair.

An honest politician's like a rose
Without a scent, I do suppose:
Find a politician who's a little bent –
He's like a rose that has some scent!
Warren – you're number one
In the galaxy of fun.

Warren hated being president
Or in the White House resident:
Too many duties, too much work –
It's enough to drive a man beserk.
Warren – you please me so,
And you let the good times flow.

But he did not fill his term,
Died in office – the facts are firm.
Then Calvin Coolidge took his place
And did his best to keep the pace.
But Warren – you're number one
In the galaxy of fun.

His speeches were renowned for length,
Though maybe grammar was not his strength.
But when I go to bed at night,
I think of Warren, who was always right.
Warren – you're number one
In the galaxy of fun.

Hero of capitalist labor

Call me Bucky Buckaroo
I got lots of bucks
I own a field of oil wells
I've had my share of luck.

I'm working sixteen hours a day
There's not much time for sleep
My cell phone runs my schedule
And I jump each time it beeps.

Vacations? I don't take them
I've got too much to do,
And if I missed a meeting
I know that I'd feel blue.

I'm making lots of money
I put it in the bank
I don't have time to spend it,
My social schedule's blank.

Call me Bucky Buckaroo
I got lots of dough
My investors all admire me,
They see their profits grow.

Call me Bucky Buckaroo
I got lots of cash
I'm working sixteen hours a day
My life's gone in a flash.

Fighting communism in the 1950s

Every Hollywood star could be a communist spy
That's why we interrogate them, to find the reason why.
It's an intricate plot, a vast conspirac—ee
That's spreading through the land, from sea to shining sea.
Read John Stormer's book and you will learn the reason
Why his title is, None Dare Call it Treason.
Every President since, Hoover Herbert J.
Was a communist spy who worked in Soviet pay.
John Birch and Robert Welch were patriotic guys
Who loved the American flag and were so very wise –
They're underneath my bed, they've occupied my barn
The communists are everywhere, please someone sound the
    alarm.
Every Senator knows that Joe McCarthy's right
That's why we've got to prosecute and turn the commies to flight.

J. Edgar Hoover's coming to town

(may be sung to the tune of "Santa Claus is coming to town")

You better not rat, you better not spy
You best not defect, I'm telling you why
J. Edgar Hoover's coming to town!
You better not rat, you better not spy
You best not defect, I'm telling you why
J. Edgar Hoover's coming to town!

He knows if you're a commie
He knows if you're a red
He knows if you are hiding
Lenin's works under your bed.

So you better watch out,
You better not spy
'cause he's got the clout
To make you cry.
J. Edgar Hoover's coming to town!
He's making a list and checking it twice,
He already knows who's naughty and nice.
J. Edgar Hoover's coming to town!

He might be in a frilly dress
He might have makeup on
But he will always catch his man,
'cause the guy is plenty strong.

You better not rat, you better not spy
You best not defect, I'm telling you why

J. Edgar Hoover's coming to town!
He's making a list and checking it twice,
He already knows who's naughty and nice.
J. Edgar Hoover's coming to town!
J. Edgar Hoover's coming to town!
J. Edgar Hoover's coming to town!

Regime changer

I'm a 21st-century Robin Hood
And I'll decide what's bad and good,
I'm a new Clark Kent and Superman,
If I want to do it, then I can.
I got X-ray vision and can see through lies,
My high-tech weapons pack a surprise.
I'm a kind of saint, I'm a Texas ranger:
My life's work is regime changer.

Regime changer, regime changer,
If I want to do it, then I can.
Regime changer, regime changer,
Just ask me, 'cause I'm the man.

I'm tired of regimes that want new missiles,
When my veep hears about it, he always bristles.
I'm tired of countries with their own religions,
They ought to say an act of contrition.
I'm tired of hearing about gay rights,
But I like seeing senators wearing tights.
I'm tired of patients who want free care,
If they don't like it here, they can go else-where.

Regime changer, regime changer,
If I want to ban it, then I can.
Regime changer, regime changer,
I make the rules, 'cause I'm the man.

We all know that only one thing can be best,
So once we know what it is, we get rid of the rest.
Variety – who needs it? We'll do it my way,
So pay close attention to what I say:
Every country on earth should be the same
Making it so – why, that's my aim.
I'm always right, and that's just so,
If you don't agree, then you're a foe.

Regime changer, regime changer,
If I want to do it, then I can.
Regime changer, regime changer,
Just ask me, 'cause I'm the man.

Take me out to the war games

(with apologies to Jack Norworth)

Take me out to the war games
Take me out to Iraq
All I want is to lead an attack
I don't care if I never come back.
Just let me fight against terror
Let's go search house to house,
For it's one, two, three bombs you're out
In the old war games!

Take me out to the war games
Take me out to Iraq
As long as we stay who says that we've lost?
We'll stay there forever no matter the cost
Just take me out to the oil fields,
Let me see Abu Ghraib,
For it's one, two, three bombs you're out
In the old war games!

Bunnies, kitties, crocodiles

Rhyme of the Ancient Bunny

Far from earth on a distant star
a bunny empress reigns,
All of her subjects stand in line
to do as she ordains.

These bunnies are the ruling class
and they control the seas,
They keep in line the throng and mass,
and do this with great ease.

The great event of every year
is carrot harvest day by chance.
This is a day of mirth and cheer,
when bunnies sing and drink and dance.

Now bunnies are a cultured breed
and pride themselves on rules
and fineries of etiquette –
for that they go to schools.

They study how to sit and stand
and when to say "excuse me,"
and when to lend a helping hand
and how to be amusing.

Their wit and talent know no bounds,
they love to praise each other.

And so they go around and 'round,
each flattering the other.

But humans – where are they, you ask!
Why, they've acquired the habit
of performing sundry menial tasks
as subjects to the rabbits.

A few, course, are placed in zoos,
for bunnies to behold.
They're safer there than on the loose,
they're safer in the fold.

You ask wherefore this "bunny rule"?
No, surely this is jest,
For it's well known to even fools
that bunny rule is best.

Sasha's song

I'm a little kitty cat
Rub my tummy and stroke my back
Let me out to look around
I'll climb a tree and hop to the ground
I'll catch some birds and chase some bees
Let me out, oh pretty please.

I'm a little kitty cat
Rub my belly and stroke my back
Feed me twice a day or more
Put my food plate on the floor.
I like tuna most of all
Feed me now and please don't stall.

I'm a little kitty cat
Rub my tummy and stroke my back
Let me sleep with you in bed
Stroke my neck and pat my head
I'll be lying on your chest –
Don't you think that's for the best?

I'm a little kitty cat
Rub my belly and stroke my back
I'm a little kitty cat
I'm the cutest on the mat.

Possible rabbits in this house

There are no rabbits in this house.
But ask a philosopher,
how many possible rabbits are there
in this house?
None, you say?
But we do not speak of real rabbits,
only of possible ones
or do you believe for a moment
that no rabbits are possible in this house?
No, you cannot say that!
There are no rabbits in this house,
but rabbits are possible.
So we ask again,
how many possible rabbits are in this house?
Sixty-three, you say?
Why not sixty-four?
Four hundred?
Why not four hundred and one?
An infinite number, you say?
Don't be silly – that is meaningless.
The correct answer is:
the number of possible rabbits in this house
cannot be determined.
Now you know.

All aboard, kitties!

(This rhyme mimics the sound of an old-fashioned train.)

The kitties decide
shorf shorf
to go for a ride
shorf shorf
they're packin' their bags
shorf shorf
and wavin' their flags
shorf shorf
ya wanna go far?
shorf shorf
a train or a car
shorf shorf
will prove to be best
shorf shorf
the kitties go west
shorf shorf
at quarter to two
shorf shorf
they line in the queue
shorf shorf
and get on the train
shorf shorf
it's startin' to rain
shorf shorf
but kitties have seats
shorf shorf
and plenty of treats

shorf shorf
like tuna and seal
shorf shorf
it's time for a meal
shorf shorf
they take in the view
shorf shorf
well, how do you do?
shorf shorf

My cat's obsession

A rubber band is jiggly,
it wiggles at the touch
I want to find a rubber band
I want that very much
I always purr when I locate
a rubber band around,
Perhaps I'll find one on the chair
or lying on the ground.
When I find a rubber band
I jump and shout, "For joy!"
I stretch my paw and play with it –
That's really fun: "Oh boy!"
I like to see them taut and stretched,
Don't think that I'm obsessed.
and when I have a rubber band
there's no way I'm depressed.

Do crocodiles have ghosts?

Now crocodiles – it is well known – always swim upstream,
this is because – I do suppose – all crocodiles do dream
of living high above the world, upon the mountain tops,
they never do descend and yet the process never stops.

And when these crocodiles expire and draw their final breath,
there is no afterlife for them – no, nothing after death.
So if you think you've seen their ghosts hovering aloof,
then be so kind and furnish me with overwhelming proof.

No, crocodiles are mortal – my friend, he says so too,
and he has seen a lot of them around the city zoo,
and if you've never seen a ghost of some dead crocodile
or seen him part his jaws to spread a Liberace smile,

then that is quite sufficient their existence to deny
'cause these are facts upon the strength of which you can rely.
And so it is I raise my glass to signify a toast
to every deceased crocodile's nonexistent ghost.

There's a rabbit in my brain

Hey doctor doctor doctor
there's a rabbit in my brain
hey doctor doctor doctor
he's driving me insane
hey doctor doctor doctor
he's talking all day long
hey doctor doctor doctor
I think there's something wrong.

Can you give me drugs to fix me up?
(now) that would be so swell
You gotta have a tablet that will work
to get me feelin' well.
Maybe there's a pill that I can take
to shut this rabbit up
He's talkin' lotsa nonsense all the time
I'm ready to give up.

Hey doctor doctor doctor
there's a rabbit in my brain
hey doctor doctor doctor
he's driving me insane
hey doctor doctor doctor
he's talking all day long
hey doctor doctor doctor
I think there's something wrong.

He's chattering away without a break
it's more than I can take,
he offers his opinions constantly –
he makes my whole brain ache.
Can you give me shots to tranquilize
this rabbit in my head?
Maybe if I take some sleeping pills,
the hare will go to bed.

Hey doctor doctor doctor
there's a rabbit in my brain
hey doctor doctor doctor
he's driving me insane
hey doctor doctor doctor
he's talking all day long
hey doctor doctor doctor
I think there's something wrong.

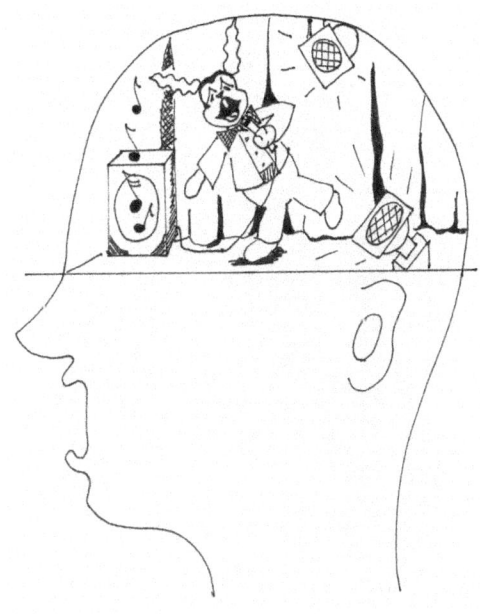

World history in rhyme

Gallia est omnis divisa

Julius Caesar knew that Gaul
had three provinces in all,
He knew they differed just a bit,
in laws and customs and clothes that fit.
He gave speeches people liked,
From miles around the people hiked
just to hear the Roman Caesar,
He was such a people pleaser.

He knew that on the floor of life,
were none as lovely as his wife,
Unless it was his mistress
Or Cleopatra, second wife.
The ship of sails, it was so big,
It tasted like a sun-baked fig,
He shared the feast with friends and foes
But made them pirouette upon their toes.

He served up banquets in his suite,
He said he wanted friends to eat,
so that they would end up fat,
and pleased in Caesar's habitat.
He gave speeches people liked,
From miles around the people hiked
just to hear the Roman Caesar,
He was such a people pleaser.

He brought Britain under Rome,
his enemies should dress in foam,
so that they could be recognized
and that he would not be surprised.
But on the Ides of March a group
of men in togas on the stoop
drew their blades and pressed their best
to draw royal blood from Caesar's chest.

So when you listen what you hear
and in your brain you hear it clear,
that Caesar wanted to be King,
Well maybe there's another thing.
Because on life are many factors,
Many roles and many actors,
Which is which is known to some,
But thinking can be cumbersome.

Upon the floor of life you find,
Plastic pigeons of a kind
that you cannot eat or feed,
Or your face on Caesar's coin you need.
But Rome, it fell – and thus to fellows,
Whose intent was aught but mellow.
Time, it's but, will not erase
the memories of in that place.

And if you think the syntax strange,
or grammar wandering off the range,
It is the meaning you should trod,
to see what's sense and what is odd.
Lest tidgets, mickles, fenesore,
Much too rorfad to ignore,
In the magic yatsoflage,
Here's a morbid haste of zage.

Hafizullah Amin's flies

Hafizullah Amin knew wherever he went
that people would turn and say, "There goes a gent."
Down in Kabul, his palace was teaming with flies
and when foreigners visited, they were surprised.
For protocol dictates that photos be made
to record the respect that the visitors paid.
But the president wanted his visitors small:
So the photos showed that he was biggest of all.
His head was blown up to be bigger by half;
for that he could thank his photography staff.
But in spite of their efforts, in spite of their tries,
they couldn't blot out every sign of the flies

Lukashenko's hippo

If you were Lukashenko, you'd have a house in Minsk
You'd have a hockey team as well, your rivals would be jinxed.
You'd have a hippopotamus that's skating on the ice.
Your hippo's name? Why, Koba! Now wouldn't that be nice!

If you were Lukashenko, you'd have a fine moustache
Your suits would be so elegant, you'd dress with such panache.
Your hockey team would always win, your hippo would rejoice.
Babies would be named for you: you'd be the people's choice.

And when there'd be elections, you know you'd always win
Your enemies would grind their teeth, but you would spread a grin.
Hippos they are heavy, they cannot jump or fly
But if you were president, then you could always try.

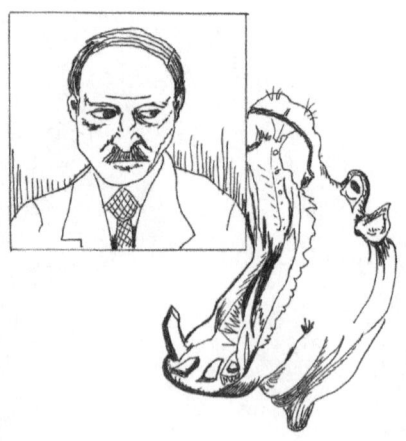

Cardinal Richelieu's cattery

(May be recited with a French accent.)

Cardinal Richelieu – he was so smart,
He knew what he wanted, right from the start.
He wanted power, he wanted cats –
Why do you doubt me? I'm telling you facts.
His cats wanted luxury, he had to comply;
So he built a huge cattery out at Versailles.
There they were waited on – daytime and night –
And enjoyed every fancy and every delight.
His cats hated Huegenots, or so he maintained;
It would not have been right if he had refrained
From administering what these heretics had earned,
Or from teaching them lessons that he had learned.
And while they were whipped and burned at the stake,
Richelieu stroked his kitties and sang for their sake,
"Knick-knack, bric-a-brac,
All my kitties dress in black.
Ping pong, sing along,
Protestants aren't here for long."

Louis the thirteenth was monarch of France,
Had a scepter and crown and a pair of silk pants.
His olfactory powers were strong and he smelled
Trouble brewing and worried that soon it would jell.
The Huegenots' faith had rotted and seemed
Most vile to him; now they plotted and schemed.
So he called on the cardinal, told him his woes,
He knew that the clergyman was on his toes.
The cardinal hired intendants and then

Consulted the cats in his cattery den.
His cats meowed and they purred and then they demanded
That all of the Huegenots had to be branded.
And while they were branded and burned at the stake,
Richelieu stroked his kitties and sang for their sake,
"Knick-knack, bric-a-brac,
All my kitties dress in black.
Ping pong, sing along,
Protestants aren't here for long."

His kitties liked knick knacks and they were so clustered
That the servants spent hours while knicks knacks were dusted.
The bric-a-brac filled every inch of the palace,
Except where the cats had their milk in a chalice
Or their golden trays laden with tuna and ham,
Laced with chicken paté and sprinkled with lamb.
There were dozens of cats being stroked half the day,
By an army of strokers working for pay.
But the cats were not patient with heretics. Thus,
They would meow most imperiously, raising a fuss,
With a cry that all Huegenots be put to the flame
In honor of heaven and King Louis's name.
And while they were whipped and burned at the stake,
Richelieu stroked his kitties and sang for their sake,
"Knick-knack, bric-a-brac,
All my kitties dress in black.
Ping pong, sing along,
Protestants aren't here for long."

Suleyman and his gazehounds go to Vienna for dinner

Suleyman was sultan and he was quite a guy,
Five-foot-six and wavy hair and sabers on each thigh.
He had a pack of gazehounds, they lived on roasted meat.
He'd trained them to do somersaults – now that was quite a feat.

And when he fancied schnitzel, he took his troops to Wien.
He laid siege to the city: his troops made quite a scene.
Yet with ropes and hooks and ladders, they couldn't scale the wall
But Suleyman liked coffee and the smell put all in thrall.

The Viennese sent word to him, "That smell is just magnificent,
And if you give us coffee, it would be so munificent."
So Suleyman decided to offer them a deal:
He would give them coffee, if they'd prepare a meal.

So everyone had schnitzel – his troops and caribou,
The eunuchs and the harem girls, and yes, the gazehounds too.
And when they had departed and gone back to whence they came,
The Viennese – they promised him an everlasting fame.

The falcons of Charles V

Knights have rights and kings have things
And knights have rights to things,
Which kings can grant when they have the mind
And exact a payment in kind.

Now Charles the Fifth ruled half the world
And had a ton of gold
But falcons they were hard to find –
At least that's what's been told.
He was the King of Sicily,
Of Naples and of Spain
He was the Roman emperor,
He ruled in his domain.

One day a group of knights
Came calling on His Highness,
With shining armor and blue plumes
They'd donned their very finest.
They told the king about themselves
About the thieves they'd hung
About the damsels they had rescued
And about the songs they'd sung.

But still they lacked a kingdom,
Without that they would falter.
They asked the king to give them one
And they suggested Malta.

King Charles the Fifth was so amused
By this request and said,
"OK, I'll give you Malta
To serve you as your stead.

But you must give me falcons,
A new one every year.
I'll feed them pigeons, ducks, and quail
And let them quaff some beer."
And so they gave him falcons,
Each year another bird,
And after four and twenty years,
He'd gathered quite a herd.

There were falcons in the choir loft,
Upon the throne and altar,
But eventually, or so they say,
There were no birds on Malta.
The Maltese falcons were all gone
To bring the king some pleasure,
But in return the Knights of Malta
Had won an earthly treasure.

Twinkle twinkle, Father Tsar

Twinkle twinkle, Father Tsar,
your Rasputin is bizarre
mystic healer or a drunk,
who knows the depths to which he'd sunk?
But in the stories that were spun,
it seems he helped the prince, your son.

While the Bolshies made their plot,
you sailed around, enjoyed your yacht.
Lenin, Trotsky, and their lot
took you for an idiot.
But you ruled quite absolute –
you were a man of known repute.

Twinkle twinkle, Father Tsar,
how I wonder what you are,
high above the world you hide,
by your people deified.
But all things come to an end,
and that's a law you don't transcend.

Twinkle twinkle, Father Tsar,
how I wonder what you are.

Enver, don't shoot

Enver Hoxha – he knew French,
he had the best seat on the bench.
He knew Shehu from the start,
abolished taxes: that was smart,
built some bunkers 'cross the land,
half a million – that was grand.
All the while he thought he knew
that Mehmet Shehu would be true.

Mehmet Shehu was a hoot!
His last words were "Enver don't shoot!"
As he loaded up his gun,
He shouted "There's just one number one."
"Enver, don't shoot! Enver, don't shoot!"
His last words were "Enver, don't shoot!"

Shehu was prime minister,
some said that he was sinister.
He was tough – now that's for sure,
For his foes, death was the cure.
Skanderbeg had a "giant mind"
or so he revealed to humankind.
Mao Zedong inspired him,
but the Little Red Book – it tired him.

Mehmet Shehu was a hoot!
His last words were "Enver don't shoot!"
As he loaded up his gun,
He shouted "There's just one number one."
"Enver, don't shoot! Enver, don't shoot!"
His last words were "Enver, don't shoot!"

Then they quarreled and they split,
Enver Hoxha threw a fit.
And when he needed a problem solver,
he just reached for his revolver.
"Mehmet Shehu, you've betrayed
the party and it's time you paid
for your independent point of view.
Now it's time to say adieu."

Mehmet Shehu was a hoot!
His last words were "Enver don't shoot!"
As he loaded up his gun,
He shouted "There's just one number one."
"Enver, don't shoot! Enver, don't shoot!"
His last words were "Enver, don't shoot!"

Enver Hoxha had decided
Shehu would be "suicided"
Shehu left a little note,
Said it was an accident and I quote,
"I cleaned my gun and took a breath,
and then it went off and caused my death."
Or maybe it was suicide,
plain and simple: you decide.

Mehmet Shehu was a hoot!
His last words were "Enver don't shoot!"
As he loaded up his gun,
He shouted "There's just one number one."
"Enver, don't shoot! Enver, don't shoot!"
His last words were "Enver, don't shoot!"

Honky-tonk Slobo

Honky-tonk Slobo sittin' at the keyboard
Honky-tonk Slobo bangin' out a tune
All the men gonna tap their feet
All the women are gonna swoon.
He's a charismatic guy
He'll make you reach for the clouds in the sky.

Slobodan Milošević – he's a Serb
He's got a pet pig he calls Herb.
Herb told the president he loved the state
And wanted to see his Serbia great:
Push the boundaries back a bit,
The international community will throw a fit
But it won't care a fig – tak-a-tak tak-a-tak
Or so thought the pig – tak-a-tak tak-a-tak.

Mirjana Marković was his friend,
Wife and lover to the bitter end.
They stroked Herb and dreamt of land
And how their Serbia would expand
And they let the Chinese in,
All of them speaking Mandarin.

Greater Serbian dreams are snuffed,
Slobodan Milošević has been rebuffed.
He was a showman, he could sing,
Herb, his pig, liked to call him "Bing".

But turbo-folk got him all confused
And new thing, he was accused
Of the crimes of war – tak-a-tak tak-a-tak
And of much much more – tak-a-tak tak-a-tak.

The red-capped cardinal and his pretty shark

Could a red-capped cardinal have a pretty pet –
A hippo or a rhino that could do a pirouette?
If you think that he could, then you might be on the mark
Though his little pet of choice was a greyish pygmy shark.

The cardinal of Esztergom, he had a pretty boat
That he kept in his palace, to sail around his moat,
But when he had the time, he took his boat to sea
And brought along his pygmy shark and let him swim out free.

So the greyish pygmy shark, it had a little swim
Around Lake Balaton to keep its figure trim,
And while it was out swimming, the cardinal reflected
Upon the holy mysteries and then he genuflected.

The trinity continued to perplex the holy man
And the virgin birth was more than he could ever understand
But his shark didn't worry about these holy creeds
And was quite content to satisfy its gustatory needs.

Saparmurat Niazov Turkmenbashi's orchard of unicorns

Turkmenbashi, man of gold, you rule a land both rich and old,
you know the thoughts in people's minds, you know that love of nation binds
children of this land as one. Who knows what deeds will yet be done?
Here's the truth I will describe: Turkmenbashi leads our tribe.

In your orchard I have seen, unicorns so strong and lean,
I have seen you thinking hard, your own pains you disregard,
while you try to find the way to lead your people from disarray.
I have seen you taking time to write inspired lines in rhyme.

Many streets are named for you, that is right, that is your due.
Our vodka bottles make some space on their labels for your face.
And when a meteor came down, landing near a Turkmen town,
You named it for yourself and stated, that it should be celebrated.

You've written moral guidelines too, which our children must read through.
You banned gold teeth and gold tooth caps, you know that those are dentists' traps.
A palace of ice should be erected, and for its location you selected
The middle of the desert plain – in Karakum, a hot domain.

You renamed all the months and days, you inspired a poetry craze,
with your insights and your wit, such as my very favorite,

"Only a Turkmen can make a Turkmen out of a Turkmen."
You asked your unicorns for advice, on how to build a paradise.

Some people want to criticize, I just want to eulogize
your noble deeds, your one-horned steeds
your posture and your choice of suits.
Count me among your loyal recruits.

(The line "Only a Turkmen can make a Turkmen out of a Turkmen" is taken from Michael Krakovskiy, "Deadprogrammerbashi", at *Deadprogrammers' Café*, at www.deadprogrammer.com/?p=1262 [accessed on 11 August 2007].)

Goebbels' Nazi turkey

He ran the propaganda,
invention was his style
But every time his turkey spoke
it made Joe Goebbels smile.

His turkey liked the minister,
he loved him very much
And always he responded
to Joe Goebbels' friendly touch.

"Goebbel, goebbel," said the turkey.
He knew no other words,
But turkey with these words was prized
above all other birds.

He sang no hymns for Himmler,
he sang no hits for Hitler,
But when Joe Goebbels came along
he chimed out "Goebbel Goebbel".

Cleopatra's sweetie

I've held Great Caesar in my arms
and relished in his manly charms
I've felt Marc Anthony's gentle kiss
but never knew such love as this.

I take my final lover now
and for the third time take a vow
that I'll be faithful to my asp
until I take my final gasp.

My sweetie snakes up to my breast
lays its head on the royal crest
and then it kisses me as lover
My reign and life will soon be over.

The golden words of Mao Zedong

(May be sung to the tune of "The yellow rose of Texas".)

I was re-educated in the time of Mao Zedong,
I memorized his Red Book and read it all day long,
Although I had a Ph.D. I worked down in a mine,
the labor helped me realize that China had it fine.

Oh the golden words of Mao Zedong are all I need to know,
they fill my life, enrich my mind and make me smile and glow,
and though it's sure that much has changed, there's much that's stayed the same,
and here I'd like to mention the chairman's well-earned fame.

A hundred flowers tried to bloom but they were mostly weeds,
there was nothing good about them – not what the country needs,
We used to have mass meetings, down in the village square,
we rounded up the landlords and explained what was unfair.

We brought out some reformers and made them wear dunce caps
and admit that their experiments had resulted in mishaps,
we had a revolution and changed the names of streets,
we dressed alike and sang good songs and managed many feats.

Oh the golden words of Mao Zedong are all I need to know,
they fill my life, enrich my mind and make me smile and glow,
and though it's sure that much has changed, there's much that's stayed the same,
and here I'd like to mention the chairman's well-earned fame.

Die gute Zeiten rollen lassen

(Verse written to remember that Otto Grotewohl was chairman of the Council of Ministers from 1949 to 1964 in the East German SED, as the communist party was called, and that local East Germans would raise their glasses of wine, in his time, with a toast, "Zum Wohl, zum Grotewohl!", meaning "To your health, to Grotewohl!, a pun on his name. In an unrelated allusion, the verse recalls that the Vikings reckoned their tax in quantities of butter.)

Hier in Leipzig vi like relax
vi like pretend vi don't pay tax,
vi pull down pants und bare our asses,
den vi raise up high our glasses
und vi shout out loud und clear:
"Ja, vi like it living hier
in our socialistic land
und singing mit de marching band.
Sure, let the good times roll,
die gute Zeiten rollen lassen!"

Tax man makes heads spin und flutter
but vi tell, "Vi pay with butter.
Vi have buckets, vi drive Wagen,
how much butter is you magen?
We're not Vikings but vi like
wenn de taxes do not hike.
Ja, vi like it living hier
in our socialistic land
und singing mit de marching band.
Sure, let the good times roll,
die gute Zeiten rollen lassen!"

Come and see our waterfall,
raise your glass and say "Zum Wohl!"
Venn you've drunk a couple glass

then you say "Zum Grotewohl!"
but you know the party's right,
this seems certain venn you're tight,
When you ready now you say
"Ich trink' zur ganzen SED!"
Now we've had some alcohol,
ja zum Wohl und Grotewohl!
Best it's time for lemon frenzy
squeeze the juice into your tea
spoon in honey, stir and sip,
just leave bisschen yet for me.

Bolsheviks vs. Mensheviks

(May be sung to the tune of "Davey Crockett, King of the Wild Frontier")

Vladimir Lenin was the workers' friend
he worked very hard to the bitter end
he spared no effort to make himself heard
his political vision – it was never blurred.
Lenin, Lenin and Trotsky
Kings of the Bolsheviks!

His plan was the biggest, his plan was the best
to take over Russia from the east to the west
"Peace, land, bread" and Kerensky out!
Every revolution means that people gonna shout.
Lenin, Lenin and Trotsky
Kings of the Bolsheviks!

But the Russian Social Democrats needed to meet
'cause their disagreements were not so discreet
Axelrod, Zasulich, Potresov too
agreed with bearded Martov and all of his crew.
Lenin, Lenin and Trotsky
Kings of the Bolsheviks!

Now Julius Martov was a Menshevik,
his whole approach made Lenin sick
he thought that anyone who came through the door
ought to be admitted to the party's inner corps.
Lenin, Lenin and Trotsky
Kings of the Bolsheviks!

But Lenin and Trotsky both knew that
you couldn't run a party with a welcome mat,
makin' revolution was a tricky case,
So cadres in the party had to show a common face.
Lenin, Lenin and Trotsky
Kings of the Bolsheviks!

So Trotsky told the Mensheviks that they could go
to the dustbin of history and join the tableau
of bankrupt lackeys who didn't have a clue
and frenzied exploiters who were really through.
Lenin, Lenin and Trotsky
Kings of the Bolsheviks!

Now Lenin and Trotsky and the Bolshevik team
worked to overthrow the old regime,
they seized the power from behind the scene
and were feted and cheered wherever they were seen.
Lenin, Lenin and Trotsky
Kings of the Bolsheviks!
Lenin, Lenin and Trotsky
Kings of the Bolsheviks!

Think of Stalin

When you lie awake at night and you find you cannot sleep
(just) think about the Five-Year Plan and Russia's giant forward leap.
When, at parties, making friends, what to talk about you ask –
why not talk of Stalin's thoughts and about the people's task?
Then at dinner, at your home, while you ingest food,
you can talk of Trotsky and his anti-Soviet brood.
After dinner, in your bed, talk of Stalin with your wife,
this can but excite you both: just think of Stalin all your life.

Borut Pahor thanks Muammar al-Qaddafi for the gift of two camels

Thank you for the camels – they're such a lovely gift,
but please, dear Brother Leader, I hope you won't get miffed,
but the camels, yes the camels, will simply have to wait
and for a little while at least, they must stay in the crate.
You see, here in Slovenia, we have to follow rules:
you surely must have read about that when you were in school,
We're sending over doctors to check that they're not ill –
but hey, just getting camels: it gives me such a thrill.
After our procedures and assuming they're OK,
you'll see that all our children will shout hip hip hurray,
'cause I'll be sitting right on top, as I pet the camel's thigh
and riding down Slovenska cesta with my head held high.

We all live on a great collective farm

(This text has been approved by the Central Committee of the Center for Poetry, Song, and Unwinding (CPSU) for use, on a voluntary basis, at all CPSU functions. It is not mandatory, under the current Five Year Plan, to sing it to the tune of the Beatles' "We all live in a yellow submarine", but monitor CPSU bulletins for updates under the next Five Year Plan.)

On our great collective farm
we love working dawn to gloam,
all our lands were communized –
so the kolkhoz is also home.

We like writing our reports
which the party always reads,
and we always work the plan,
'til a new one supersedes.

We all live on a great collective farm,
a great collective farm, a great collective farm,
we all live on a great collective farm,
it really has its charm, the great collective farm.

What we plant – it has been planned
by the wisest of humankind,
all the knowledge of our land
has been poured into planners' minds.

Down at GOSPLAN they know all,
which is why ther're no mistakes,
and if you think there were mistakes,
you belong with Trotsky's snakes.

GOSPLAN knows what we ought to plant and sow,
we ought to plant and sow, we ought to plant and sow,

GOSPLAN knows what we ought to plant and sow,
it's good that they foreknow what we ought to plant and sow.

MTS has chaser bins
it has tractors and swathers too,
it has harrows and yellow balers,
it has everything for me and you.

We don't need to own our tools,
we don't need equipment – no!
MTS is all we need,
The party tells us and so we know.

We all live on a great collective farm,
a great collective farm, a great collective farm,
we all live on a great collective farm,
it really has its charm, the great collective farm.

Poems

War with the Tsar of Russia

In seventeen hundred and sixty-eight
The Sultan Mustafa could no longer wait,
So he sent his troops out through Istanbul's gate
For a war with the tsar of Russia.

He thought an alliance with Poles would serve
To boost the morale of his men and unnerve
The Russians who'd sworn to always observe
The decrees of the tsar of Russia.

But Suvurov defeated the Poles on land
While at sea too the Turkish fleet could not withstand
The fleet under Admiral Orlov's command
Who brought triumph to the tsar of Russia.

The Russians and Turks signed a treaty of peace
Which called for the combat and fighting to cease
With Crimea assigned to the Russians on lease,
For His Highness the tsar of Russia.

Iskandar rise!

The threats we face,
the fast decline,
the scale and scope
of our misfortunes,
of our dread –
how will we cope?
We cling to hope:
Iskandar rise!

Our riches squandered,
our forests stripped,
our energy spent,
our young men lost
in pointless wars
to which they were sent,
never to return from where they went.
Iskandar rise!

A hero's born
with noble heart
and piercing mind.
He grows, he learns,
the best solution we know he'll find,
and when he comes, he'll save our kind.
Iskandar rise!

Justice

Still. Cold. Stiff. Departed.
God's grace has imparted
this soul with salvation,
rich gift of creation.
All good folk rewarded,
rot and filth accorded
what's their due – damnation.
God is just – prostration.
If you show contrition,
you may pass perdition.
Through Him find direction.
God is this: perfection.

The extinction (2007)

High on a rocky crevice once
a cunning bird was bred,
that fed on other living beasts
and also on the dead.
No condor could fly higher,
no hawk had keener sight,
and when it swooped like a vulture
'twas too late to take flight.
But then came hunters out for "sport"
who took aim at their prey,
they thought that birds would look nice stuffed
and put out on display.
So one by one the breed died out,
no specimens remain.
The barren skies are silent now,
to protest is in vain.

Absolute Cheese

I was walking in the park and I saw some cheese,
And I asked it, "Are you Absolute Cheese?"
But the cheese, a fine slice of Appenzeller,
Said to me,
"No, there is no absolute cheese,
Only various kinds of cheese.
I am an Appenzeller,
But I am not a cheddar or a cream cheese,
Or a single Gloucester,
Let alone a Double Gloucester."
I looked at the path on which I was standing,
And I looked at the trees,
And then I let my gaze drop again
Until I was looking once more at the cheese,
And I said,
"I am looking for Absolute Cheese,
And I thought that I would find it in this park.
This is so nice a place, so leafy, so green,
And I feel so full of hope.
And when I hope, I hope for cheese,
Oh please…"
But it was to no avail. The cheese scampered away,
Perhaps to join a sandwich
Or to grace an omelet with its fine aroma.
Ah cheese-friend, you please me so…

Real joy

The smell of asphalt in the spring
is what makes me want to sing,
simply that can always bring
real joy

the sound that alligators make
swimming in a stream or lake,
that's a sound that takes the cake:
real joy

the feel of cold cathedral walls
or of the spray from waterfalls,
the turgid air in abandoned halls:
real joy.

Reggae

Ba-ba-daah

Down in Jamaica in Kingston town
coconut shells grow thick and brown
If you drink lots of coconut milk
your whole body gonna feel like silk
Ba-ba-daah, ba-ba-daah
Ba-ba-daah, ba-ba-daah

Then in the evening you feel like a twirl
Call to the matron and she send you a girl,
You can dance and sing 'til the sky grow pale
'n' you're gonna tell a pretty tale
Ba-ba-daah, ba-ba-daah
Ba-ba-daah, ba-ba-daah

If you wanna be King of the bush,
shake your shoulders and swing your tush,
just don't forget that I tell you that
you better off stayin' home on the mat
Ba-ba-daah, ba-ba-daah
Ba-ba-daah, ba-ba-daah
Ba-ba-daah, ba-ba-daah
Ba-ba-daah, ba-ba-daah…

Reggae archaeologicae

I dig all night, I dig all day
I dig through dirt, I dig through clay
What do I find? I find more dirt
Hey you there! I'm no per-vért!
I just like digging 'cause once I found
something exciting stuck in the ground.
I picked it up, what did I see?
Why it was some kinda big brass key –
Now where there's a key, there must be a door
for me what does fate now hold in store?
I looked many years, looked everywhere,
but found no door lying anywhere,
So I gave up the search but not the dig,
and then I found a thingamajig!
It wasn't a door but a piece of vase,
or maybe a chip of a statue's face,
or maybe the edge of a blackbird's wing,
but whatever it was, it made me sing!
Sometimes the years roll by in tens,
with finding nothing – work's intense,
But I tell myself, "you don't despair,
though I chew my nails and bite my hair."
And then success and worldwide fame,
everyone gonna know my name,
'cause I'm the one who found this thing,
to which I've tied a little string.

I know I'm handsome and you wanna flirt,
but all I wanna do is dig in the dirt.
I dig a hole and climb below:
I'm an archaeolo-gíst you know,
I'm living every childhood dream,
this is glory raised supreme.

Social commentary & ordinary life

The whole world's an ashtray

(May be sung to the tune of "St. James' Infirmary")

The whole world's an ashtray
I spread my ash around,
I stick my butt into the ground
Man, that sure feels good.

When I chew gum and when I'm done
I spit it on the street
And when there's gum between my feet,
Man, that sure feels neat.

And when I feel saliva
buildin' up inside my mouth,
I know there's one solution:
gotta gotta spit it out.

The whole world's an ashtray –
cigarette butts and gum and spit,
and when you stop and think about it,
Man, that sure feels good.

Forms

A giant wave swells up of bureaucratic forms,
with rules and new procedures and explicated norms.
I'm climbing to the top of it and try to ride the wave,
but my pen is not a surfboard, so I'm waiting to be saved.
Then, who is that? – it's Zorro!, with cape and mask and sword,
He rescues me and grabs the forms and throws them overboard.
I'll fill them out tomorrow – of that I'm very sure,
but now – today – I'm happy with a temporary cure.

At the chemist's

I'm not looking for some thrills,
just some anti-headache pills,
and some tablets I can take
so that I don't stay awake
all night long when I should sleep,
I want slumber – long and deep.
Also, if you've some to spare,
give me pills to grow some hair.
pills pills pills pills
pills pills pills pills
When I get a stomach ache,
there's a tablet I can take,
when I'm dizzy in the head,
I can take a pill and go to bed,
when my ears begin to ring –
for that there is another thing.
And when I have a pain-free day
I take some pills to stay that way.
pills pills pills pills
pills pills pills pills…

Pleasantville, USA

(Any resemblance to any town which might or might not be known as Pleasantville, whether it is located somewhere or somewhere else, is purely unintentional)

In happy Pleasantville you'll find
each household has a boat
to sail around in circles
in each household's private moat.
You won't find lakes or rivers
for many miles around,
altho' you'll find a lot of ships
that must have run aground.
In Pleasantville the folks have phones
that are quite out of date,
'cause though they've tried a million times,
they can't call out of state.
The phones work best within the town
with neighbors who live near,
and sometimes even calls within
the state may be quite clear.
But calls come in from 'round the world –
no problems there we see,
let Pleasantville be Pleasantville
where everyone feels free.
From Monday down to Friday
the people go to work,
as butcher, baker, candle-maker,
fireman, or clerk.
But weekends are a time for rest,
excursions and for fun,
or sitting on the sofa

with the TV sports turned on.
There's always time to mow the lawn
and wash your pet dog's fur
or take your cat onto your lap
and listen to him purr.
And Sunday night you stroll on down
to meet up with your ilk,
you find the bar and grab a chair
and order dairy milk,
'cause that's what folks are drinkin' now
in Pleasantville these days,
and it's not likely very soon
that they will change their ways.

Stopgap, Kansas

More than a truck stop, less than a town,
Stopgap, Kansas, got it all
got a wayside chapel and a fillin' pump
got a general store at the shoppin' mall
got a bowlin' alley and cinema flicks,
at the handyman store you can buy your bricks.

On Saturday evening you can mosey on down,
put on your skates and skate aroun'.
More than a truck stop, less than a town,
Stopgap, Kansas got it all –
If you think I'm kiddin', jess take a look,
here in Stopgap have a ball!

Building without mold

So you wanted a building that has no mold –
well, this is something we should have been told
'cause our standard contract is written very plain,
that we're entitled to build in the rain.
And that means mold inside your walls,
insidious slime that creeps and crawls,
puffy fungus that blows in the air,
little mold spores that get in your hair.
If that's not something you were inclined
to want to see, you shouldn't have signed
our standard contract – no, no, no!
you should have requested something apropos.

For triple the price we guarantee
to use materials of high quali-tée
rather than the flimsy cardboard fill
you get with the standard contract quadrille.
For triple the price we'll really try
to do some building when it's dry,
and Mr. Mold will also suffer
if we use our special anti-mold buffer.
But pay attention, please take note
and here I need to read a quote:
right in the special contract read,
"Workers may take the vacation they need."
So yes, we promise that we'll try
to work construction when it's dry,

but that's just if we're not away
soaking up the sun in old Calais.

But we offer a super-special contract too
in which we pledge the entire crew
will give priority to your need
and that our vacations don't supersede:
For six times the posted price you get
a mold-free building with nothing wet.
If that's what you want, let's be precise,
say what you want and pay our price.
We're sorry of course that many of you
have gotten sick with a fungus-flu,
but in the fine print it specifies
we're not responsible if anyone dies –
'cause you wanted mold – that's clear to us,
So we don't see why you raise a fuss.
But good, let's tear the building down
and start afresh with something sound,
we're sure you will be satisfied.
So let's get serious, you decide.

A sunset on velvet

A sunset on velvet – now what can compare?
with a painting produced with such scrupulous care?
Each household should have 57 or more,
they'll go very well with your style and décor.
Find a Hawaiian shirt that you can wear,
put on your straw hat, relax in your chair,
stare at the velvet, it's lovely to view:
raises your spirits whenever you're blue.

Can a comrade be a gentleman?

Can a comrade be a gentleman
or can she be a lady?
The very notion might appear
suspicious, even shady.
A gentleman, most certainly,
must wear a coat and tie,
and say "excuse me", "even so"
and sometimes "my oh my!"
A lady – let me be quite clear –
must wear a skirt or dress
and say "why thank you", "you're so dear"
and "my, I do confess."
But comrades do not talk like that
or put on ties or skirts,
They're decked in pants and tennis shoes
and wearing open shirts.
They shout "Hail revolution!"
and "Down with exploitation!"
They want to save the working class
and unify the nation.

The Shakespeare section

Who was it what wrote Shakespeare?

Who was it what wrote Shakespeare 'cause I know it wasn't him,
maybe it was Marlowe or maybe Bowie Jim
'cause Bowie had a hunter's knife so he could cut and parse
and with it he could slice away any excess farce.
Or maybe it was Bacon – Francis or his son
or maybe was his brother or even Bacon's mum,
or maybe it was Hemingway or Scott Fitzgerald's twin
or maybe there was several, each writer chipping in.
I think it was a foreigner what wrote all Shakespeare's plays
'cause his English sounds so funny – it leaves me in a daze,
or maybe it was aliens from inner-outer space
who vowed to give some entertainment to the human race,
or maybe it was monkeys with an awful lot of time
I've heard that in a trillion years the chimps can write in rhyme.
Or maybe it was Shakespeare, a bashful man and quiet,
who thought he'd have a little fun and thought that he would try it
to circulate these rumors to make our thinking dim,
about who wrote these plays of his but maybe it was him!

Breakfast with Shakespeare

I'm lookin' at the milk carton,
Seein' who's missin' this week,
And what's the offer
On the back of the corn flakes box.
The toast is hot, fresh jam and coffee,
I think I'll have my breakfast now.
We're talkin' about Shakespeare,
That guy who wrote "Pericles"
And other stuff. *Pass the pancakes please.*
He and Chaucer were brothers, I think.
No they weren't, they had different last names
So what, maybe they were half-brothers
Or maybe Chaucer changed his name
So people wouldn't confuse them,
'course Chaucer was dead 164 years
Before Shakespeare was born – the coffee's cold –
And they had different parents – is there any OJ?
How do you know? Are you an expert on English writers?
Come on, what woman can give birth to two guys
221 years apart?
Remember Melchisedec, in the Bible? He lived more than 900 years,
And he had only one wife – so she must have lived about that long too.
You're takin' that literally? Sure, it's in the Bible!
It's an exaggeration, no one lives that long,
Look, it's in the Bible, and until you prove otherwise,

I'm assuming that people were healthier in the old days
So Chaucer and Shakespeare could have had the same mom and dad.
Whatever...
So they could've been brothers.
We're talkin' about Shakespeare
Livin' up in Stratford-upon-Avon –
Never been there:
I hear you can get a great English breakfast
In Stratford-upon-Avon.
Please pass the butter.
Or maybe it was Shakespeare what changed his name.

Hamlet's soliloquy, revised & in rhyme

I'm not sure if it's better to hang around and be
Or is there something somewhere that I'd like to see?
Or whether to engage myself in fighting endless schemes,
From all my foes and enemies or just enjoy some dreams?
If I could just lie down a while and get some sleep and snore,
Then all my nagging problems would trouble me no more,
And sitting here in Elsinore, Denmark's bustling hub,
I've got to say that that alone is nearly quite the rub.
To be or not to be around all dressed in fancy clothes
And strutting up and down the hall and striking up a pose,
It might be somewhat better than worrying too much,
'cause worry can, as we all know, serve as the devil's crutch.
And now I think I'm going to drink a brimming cup of tea
And try to figure out whether it is better not to be,
But when I think of those dead kings who made great sacrifice,
I know that one and all of them are now in paradise.

What if Shakespeare never was

What if William Shakespeare'd been
riding on a submarine
while he wrote his Cymbeline?
Would it have been anodyne?

What if he had lived in France,
and worn Parisian shirts and pants,
and wanted to excel in dance,
and meditated in a trance?

What if Shakespeare never was –
this I'm telling you because
this alone should give you pause
when next you want to give applause.

Oh, Shakespeare was a poet

(This verse may be sung to the tune of "Stewball", a song written by John Herald, Bob Yellen, and Ralph Rinzler, and sung by the popular folk group, Peter, Paul and Mary, beginning in the 1960s)

Oh, Shakespeare was a poet (ba-da ba-da, ba-da ba-da)
and he wrote lots of plays (ba-da ba-da, ba-da ba-da)
He worked in the theater (ba-da ba-da, ba-da ba-da)
to the end of his days (ba-da ba-da, ba-da ba-da).

He wrote a play "Hamlet" (ba-da ba-da, ba-da ba-da),
it dealt with a prince (ba-da ba-da, ba-da ba-da),
whose father was murdered (ba-da ba-da, ba-da ba-da):
it made Hamlet wince (ba-da ba-da, ba-da ba-da).

"The Merchant of Venice" (ba-da ba-da, ba-da ba-da)
was also his work (ba-da ba-da, ba-da ba-da),
The case of poor Portia (ba-da ba-da, ba-da ba-da) –
it drives me berserk (ba-da ba-da, ba-da ba-da).

"Macbeth" is another (ba-da ba-da, ba-da ba-da),
it has lots of blood (ba-da ba-da, ba-da ba-da),
the play has a murder (ba-da ba-da, ba-da ba-da)
and ends with a thud (ba-da ba-da, ba-da ba-da).

He also wrote "Falstaff" (ba-da ba-da, ba-da ba-da)
'bout a corpulent knight (ba-da ba-da, ba-da ba-da)
and Verdi wrote music (ba-da ba-da, ba-da ba-da)
that still can excite (ba-da ba-da, ba-da ba-da).

He wrote more than twenty (ba-da ba-da, ba-da ba-da),
including "King Lear" (ba-da ba-da, ba-da ba-da),
His plays still entrance us (ba-da ba-da, ba-da ba-da),
yes, year after year (ba-da ba-da, ba-da ba-da).

Hey, Shakespeare was a poet (ba-da ba-da, ba-da ba-da)
and he wrote lots of plays (ba-da ba-da, ba-da ba-da)
He worked in the theater (ba-da ba-da, ba-da ba-da)
to the end of his days (ba-da ba-da, ba-da ba-da).

For the young at heart

Lions and tigers

Lions and tigers sleep all day
They don't have to work for pay
They just lie around and snore
Then they turn and sleep some more.

Horses and donkeys like the ground,
Since they want to trot around
They're not going any-where,
They're just happy being there.

Otters and beavers like to swim
That's the way they stay so trim,
They will also dam up streams
Working in their day-shift teams.

Bunnies and weasels are big friends,
They share lettuce and carrot ends,
They can dance and they can sing,
They can do most anything.

Utensils

The fork met the knife
and said please be my wife,
and let us get married in church
but knife fancied the spoon
and they made honeymoon
and left the fork out in the lurch.

A lesson about life

Deep in the woods there lives an elf
He's twice as strong as he is himself.
If you're inclined to think I'm wrong,
Just take a look: you'll see he's strong.

Up on the hill there lives a crow:
Whatever he knows just isn't so.
Whatever he thinks will not make sense –
He's served in seven governments.

Jacket and sweater

The man with the jacket
created a racket,
the man with the sweater
behaved so much better.

The man with the jacket
was weary and seated,
with bowtie and shirt and
fine pants that were pleated.

He rose with a glower
and stood like a tower,
then started his pouting
and yelling and shouting.

The man with the sweater,
behaving much better,
just watched as this fellow
continued to bellow.

He couldn't help blinking
while sitting there thinking
how he was behaving
while th'other was raving.

And then he decided
that if he confided
his secret for mirth
then the shouts might subside.

So sweater told jacket
"There's no joy in racket.
It's much more beguiling
to spend your life smiling."

And then the clouds parted,
a thunderstorm started,
but jacket and sweater
were both feeling better.

A storm does not matter
when friends start to chatter –
these two men were sharing
a bench and comparing

the lessons they'd learned
and the battle scars earned
and what life had given
on paths they had driven.

Today they are friends, so
please don't be too shocked
if you should see them
arm in arm locked.

Recipe for Wiener Schnitzel

Pound the pig-meat til it's flat
clean away the excess fat
soak it then in full-fat milk
til the pig-meat's soft as silk,
then you bread it on each side
while you slice some lemons wide.
Fry the meat in olive oil
while the spuds come to a boil,
serve it up with soup and beets.
Call your friends – it's time to eat.

Something in my nose

What have I here inside my nose?
It's something nice, I do suppose,
I shouldn't let it go to waste,
And so I take a little taste!

A little story

Once upon a time
in a remote corner of the Pacific Ocean
there was a small island,
that was divided in two by a ridge of mountains.
On the Western half of the island
was the Kingdom of Tip
and on the eastern half,
the Republic of Top.
The Tippers were very proud
of being Tippers,
they said they were the best tippers
in the world,
especially in restaurants.
The Toppers were likewise a proud people,
and said that no one could be
on top of a Topper.
The Tippers were also proud
that they had a king
and no parliament,
while the Toppers
were proud of having a parliament and no king.
The Tippers mocked the Toppers
because "top" rhymes with "slop",
the Toppers mocked the Tippers
because "tip" rhymes with "slip".
Then one day,
 a mountain-eating eggplant

simply ate the mountains
which had been separating
Tippers and Toppers.
Now the Tippers and Toppers found
that they did not know
who was a Tipper and who was a Topper,
and moreover,
that they liked the same songs.
So they decided to unite
into one country
and to compromise
by agreeing to have a half-king,
alongside half of the previous parliament of Top.
They called their country "Tip Top"
and that is exactly
how the people of Tip Top felt
about it all. And they all lived happily
ever after.

Said the thrush to the shrew

How do you do
said the thrush to the shrew,
I'm doing fine
said the shrew on the vine.
If you would like
to go off on a hike,
Just fold back your wings
and pack up your things.

Dandelions

There is something I have found:
dandelions in the ground,
You can launch a fierce attack:
dandelions come right back.

Love birds

Here are love birds – they are fine,
they fly over the ocean brine,
Here are love hares – they are nice,
they like carrots with some spice.
Here are love mice, they are cool,
when they smile, they sometimes drool,
Here are love bats, hip hooray,
wishing you a happy day!

The expectorator

Here he comes – the expectorator,
So much saliva is no facilitator,
Spittin' on the street and in the elevator,
I'm steppin' forward as his castigator.

How absurd

How absurd
that the bird
flew so high
in the sky
that it flew
where it knew
there was not
to be got
such to eat
as was meet
to be found
on the ground
but it chose
sweet repose.
So it goes.

If you smile
for a while
and you sing
everything
and you dance –
sweet romance –
you'll have friends
from all ends.
You can gaze
in the haze,
to discern
and to learn
what is what
and what's not.
So it goes.

The Washington D. C. metro system

In Zanzibar I found
a pile of speckled fish.
I salted them, I peppered them,
I served them on a dish.

Ingesting all I served,
in nibbly little bites,
my guests all praised my cooking,
'cause friendship knows no heights.

They loosened their green belts,
the women and the men,
and found the door and strutted out
to find a forest glen.

And then they waved goodbye
and waddled past the stove,
their foggy bottoms swayed
'til they found a shady grove.

Marches are what life's about

The colonel came and shouted out
"Marches are what life's about,
Blow the bugle, bang the gong,
We like marching all day long."
    Sound off, one two, sound off, three four
    Sound off, one two....three four!
"Left foot, right foot, column right,
We'll be marching through the night,
When the sun pops up again,
We'll be back with this refrain:"
    Sound off, one two, sound off, three four
    Sound off, one two....three four!

 "We have uniforms and caps,
Around our feet we're wearing chaps,
We're the happy new recruits,
Showing off our shiny boots."
    Sound off, one two, sound off, three four
    Sound off, one two....three four!
"We like marching, yes we do,
Or rowing in the camp canoe,
Marches are what life's about,
That is why we love to shout:
Give us orders, we'll obey,
Happy and without dismay."
    Sound off, one two, sound off, three four
    Sound off, one two....three four!

www.ingramcontent.com/pod-product-compliance
Lightning Source LLC
Chambersburg PA
CBHW032255150426
43195CB00008BA/469